Stitch B⦿X

KNITTING MADE EASY

Contents

Welcome...

to Stitch Box *Knitting Made Easy*, a box full of surprises for all knitters, from beginners to those already hooked!

In each box you will receive a fantastic illustrated guide to help you learn or perfect basic knitting techniques, along with detailed step by step instructions for a range of exciting projects.

You will also find four balls of yarn which you will use to knit – square by square – a beautiful, colourful and modern blanket, along with yarn specially selected by our experts which will allow you to make one of the two projects offered in the "kit of the month"

This month, you will be using your four balls (periwinkle blue, hot pink, dove grey and white) to learn to knit four new squares of your blanket: one square in ladder stitch, one square in garter stitch, one square in pennant (flag) stitch and one square in broken rib stitch and stocking stitch.

With your additional balls of blue marl yarn you can choose to make a cosy muff and matching hat, or a Christmas stocking!

Stitch Box *Knitting Made Easy* offers you the pleasure of discovery, the joy of learning, and the chance to make beautiful creations quickly and with ease.

You can find all this information, along with tutorials and advice from our experts, on our website www.stitch-box.com, on our YouTube channel, and on our Facebook page.

Welcome to Stitch Box *Knitting Made Easy* and...

Let's get knitting!

Muff and *matching hat*

Wrap up **warm** this winter with these **cosy** knits!

DIMENSIONS

The finished muff measures 30cm long and 20cm wide.

The hat is one size and measures 24cm tall.

TENSION

15 rows of 10 stitches knitted in 2x2 rib on 8mm needles should measure 10 cm x 10cm.

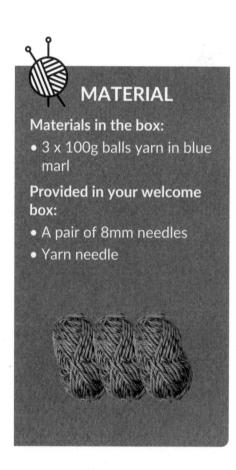

MATERIAL

Materials in the box:
- 3 x 100g balls yarn in blue marl

Provided in your welcome box:
- A pair of 8mm needles
- Yarn needle

HOW TO MAKE THE MUFF AND HAT

Muff

- Cast on 48 stitches onto 8mm needles.
- **Row 1:** (RS) Edge st, *k2, p2,* repeat from * to * until 1 last st, edge st.
- **Row 2-39:** As for Row 1.
- Work should now measure 30cm long.
- Cast off in the following row. Cut and weave in ends.

MAKING UP

Fold the rectangle in two, RS together, to form a tube 30cm long and 20cm wide. Join seams using backstitch, working into the selvedge stitches at the start and end of the rows. Turn the muff right-side out.

NEED HELP?

Consult our handy *Getting Started guide* or visit our website at **www.stitch-box.com** for all the tutorials and advice you might need to help you with your knitting projects.

Hat

- Cast on 50 stitches onto 8 mm needles.
- **Row 1:** Edge st, *k2, p2*, rep from * to * until 1 st rem, edge st.
- **Row 2-25:** Work as for row 1.
- The piece should now measure 30 cm long.
- **Row 26:** Edge st, *k2tog, p2,* rep from * to * until 1 st rem, edge st. [38 sts].
- **Row 27:** Edge st, *k2tog, p1,* rep from * to * until 1 st rem, edge st. [26 sts].
- **Rows 28-29:** Edge st, *k1, p1,* rep from * to * until 1 st rem, edge st.
- **Row 30:** Edge st, *k1, k2tog,* rep from * to * until 1 st rem, edge st. [18 sts].
- **Row 31:** P every st.
- **Row 32:** Edge st, * k1, k2tog,* rep from * to * until 1 st rem, edge st. [13 sts].
- **Row 33:** P every st.
- **Row 34:** (K2tog) 6 times, k. [7 sts].
- Cut the yarn, leaving enough length to pass the end through the remaining stitches. Pull to tighten. Pass the remaining end through to the WS of the work and weave in.

MAKING UP

Fold the hat in half, RS together. Starting at the bottom, join the side seam with backstitch, working into the selvedge stitches at the row ends. Turn right-side out.

EDGE STITCH

Create a neat edge, or selvedge, by working the first and last stitch of each row in a particular way. There are various options for this, but here, why not try a seam edge: k the first and last st on every RS row, and p the first and last st on the WS.

The 2x2 rib pattern is eye catching and looks just as good on the inside as on the outside!

For all the abbreviations please refer to the *Practical Guide* on p.52.

Christmas *Stocking*

This **large stocking** will look **perfectly festive** stuffed with presents, whether hung over the fireplace or placed under the Christmas tree!

MATERIAL

Materials in the box:

- 3 x 100g balls yarn in blue marl

Provided in your welcome box:

- A pair of 10mm knitting needles
- Yarn needles

DIMENSIONS

The finished stocking measures 30cm long, 20cm wide at the opening, and 35cm wide at the foot.

TENSION

13 rows of 8 stitches knitted in stocking stitch with 10mm needles should measure 10cm x 10cm.

MAKING THE CHRISTMAS STOCKING

The stocking is made in 2 halves, which mirror one another. They are made from the foot up.

First side

- Cast on 21 stitches onto 10mm needles.
- **Row 1:** K.
- **Row 2:** P, inc 2 at the end of the row. [23 sts].
- **Row 3:** K, inc 2 at the end of the row. [25 sts].
- **Row 4:** P, inc 2 at the end of the row. [27 sts].
- **Row 5:** K, inc 1 at the end of the row. [28 sts].
- **Row 6:** P, inc 1 at the end of the row. [29 sts].
- **Row 7:** K, inc 1 at the end of the row. [30 sts].
- **Row 8:** P.
- **Row 9:** K1, k2tog, k to end of row. [29 sts].
- **Rows 10, 12, 14, 16, 18 and 20:** P.
- **Row 11:** Cast off (CO) first 3 sts kwise, k to end. [26 sts].
- **Row 13:** CO first 3 sts kwise, k to end. [23 sts].
- **Row 15:** CO first 2 sts kwise, k to end. [21 sts].
- **Row 17:** K1, k2tog, k to end. [20 sts].
- **Row 19:** K1, k2tog, k to end. [19 sts].
- **Row 21:** K1, k2tog, k to end. [18 sts].
- **Rows 22-34:** Continue in stocking stitch.
- **Rows 35-43:** Work in garter st (k every row).
- Cast off in the following row. Cut yarn and weave in end.

Second side

- Cast on 21 stitches onto 10mm needles.
- **Row 1:** K.
- **Row 2:** P, inc 2 at the end of the row. [23 sts].
- **Row 3:** K, inc 2 at the end of the row. [25 sts].
- **Row 4:** P, inc 1 at the end of the row. [26 sts].
- **Row 5:** K, inc 2 at the end of the row. [28 sts].
- **Row 6:** P, inc 1 at the end of the row. [29 sts].
- **Row 7:** K, inc 1 at the end of the row. [30 sts].
- **Row 8:** P.
- **Row 9:** K to last 3 sts, k2tog, k1. [29 sts].
- **Row 10:** CO first 3 sts pwise, p to end. [26 sts].
- **Rows 11, 13, 15, 17, 19 and 21:** K.
- **Row 12:** CO first 3 sts pwise, p to end. [23 sts].
- **Row 14:** CO first 2 sts pwise, p to end. [21 sts].
- **Row 16:** P1, p2tog, p to end. [20 sts].
- **Row 18:** P1, p2tog, p to end. [19 sts].
- **Row 20:** P1, p2tog, p to end. [18 sts].
- **Rows 22 to 34:** Continue in stocking stitch.
- **Rows 35-43:** Work in garter stitch (k every row).
- Cast off in the following row. Cut yarn and weave in end.

MAKING UP

Lay the one side on top of the other, WS together, and pin the edges in place. Using a tapestry needle threaded with the same wool, sew around the edges of the stocking, hemming the two sides together, using blanket stitch (see box-out).

Make a plait approximately 20 cm long using three 40-cm lengths of yarn. Bring the two ends together, and attach them to the inside of the opening, at the back of the stocking.

This loop can be used to hang your stocking.

KNITTING SOS

Adding multiple stitches at the end of the row can be done a number of ways – either by working multiple times (kfb, pfb) into the last two (or more) stitches, by a combination of M1 and k or pfb, or by casting on the required number of stitches.

NEED HELP?

Consult our handy *Getting Started guide* or visit our website at **www.stitch-box.com** for all the tutorials and advice you might need to help you with your knitting projects.

TOP TIP

Blanket stitch

Bring the thread out at point A. Make a stitch at point B, pulling the thread to the right. Bring the tip of the needle out at point C, to the right of A and underneath B. Slide the thread under the needle and gently pull to finish the stitch.

The base of the scallop loops should lie neatly along the outside edge.

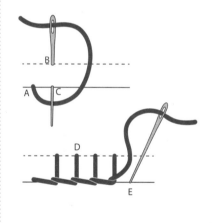

Accrochez votre botte grâce à cette attache.

For all the abbreviations please refer to the *Practical Guide* on p.52.

Your throw
square by square

Your 4 new squares to make:

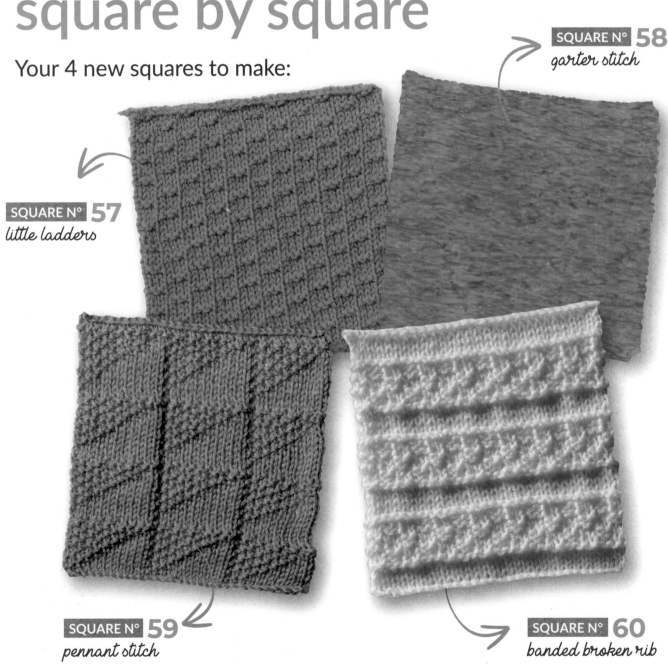

SQUARE N° 58
garter stitch

SQUARE N° 57
little ladders

SQUARE N° 59
pennant stitch

SQUARE N° 60
banded broken rib

Square n°57
little ladders

Here is another **ladder stitch** square, this time in a **gorgeous shade** of blue.

MATERIALS

Materials in the box:

- 1 x ball of perinwinkle yarn (save any leftover for future squares)

Provided in your welcome box:

- A pair of 4mm knitting needles

NEED HELP?

Consult our handy *Getting Started guide* or visit our website at **www.stitch-box.com** for all the tutorials and advice you might need to help you with your knitting projects.

DIMENSIONS

The finished square measures approx 15 x 15cm.

TENSION

22 stitches and 32 rows over 10cm square pattern on 4mm needles.

For the best results it is important that you work to stated tension.

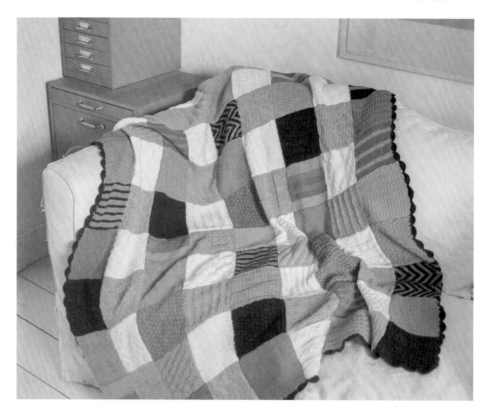

HOW TO KNIT THE SQUARE

- Cast on 34 sts with 4mm needles.
- **Row 1:** (RS) k to end.
- **Row 2:** P4, *k2, p4, rep from * to end.
- **Row 3:** K to end.
- **Row 4:** *P1, k2, p3, rep from * to last 4 sts, p1, k2, p1.
- These 4 rows form patt. Rep them until work measures 15cm from beg, ending with a WS row.
- Cast off knitwise, working into the back of each st.

MAKING UP

Place the square on a flat, padded surface and ease out to correct dimensions, pinning around edges if necessary. Cover with a clean, lightly dampened cloth and leave until square and cloth are dry. Store the square flat until you are ready to sew the throw together.

For all the abbreviations please refer to the *Practical Guide* on p.52.

TOP TIP

Store the square flat until you are ready to assemble your throw, pin a small piece of paper with the square number on to the square. This will allow you to find your way more easily during the final assembly of your throw.

15

Square n°58
garter stitch

You should be able to knit this **hot pink** square in **double-quick** time by now!

MATERIALS

Materials in the box:

- 1 x ball of hot pink yarn (save any leftover for future squares)

Provided in your welcome box:

- A pair of 4mm knitting needles

NEED HELP?

Consult our handy *Getting Started guide* or visit our website at **www.stitch-box.com** for all the tutorials and advice you might need to help you with your knitting projects.

HOW TO KNIT THE SQUARE

- ❤ Cast on 33 sts with 4mm needles.

- ❤ **1st row:** (RS) k to end.

- ❤ Rep last row throughout to form g st until work measures 15cm from beg.

- ❤ Cast off knitwise working into the back of each st.

MAKING UP

Place the square on a flat, padded surface and ease out to correct dimensions, pinning around edges if necessary. Cover with a clean, lightly dampened cloth and leave until square and cloth are dry. Store the square flat until you are ready to sew the throw together.

TOP TIP

Store the square flat until you are ready to assemble your throw, pin a small piece of paper with the square number on to the square. This will allow you to find your way more easily during the final assembly of your throw.

For all the abbreviations please refer to the *Practical Guide* on p.52.

DIMENSIONS

The finished square measures approx 15 x 15cm.

TENSION

22 stitches and 44 rows in patt over 10cm square on 4mm needles.

For the best results it is important that you work to stated tension.

Square n°59
pennant stitch

Alternating **moss stitch** and **stocking stitch** triangles form this square.

MATERIALS

Materials in the box:

- 1 x ball of dove grey yarn (save any leftover for future squares)

Provided in your welcome box:

- A pair of 4mm knitting needles

NEED HELP?

Consult our handy *Getting Started guide* or visit our website at **www.stitch-box.com** for all the tutorials and advice you might need to help you with your knitting projects.

DIMENSIONS

The finished square measures approx 15 x 15cm.

TENSION

22 stitches and 32 rows over 10cm square pattern on 4mm needles.

For the best results it is important that you work to stated tension.

TOP TIP

Store the square flat until you are ready to assemble your throw, pin a small piece of paper with the square number on to the square. This will allow you to find your way more easily during the final assembly of your throw.

HOW TO KNIT THE SQUARE

- Cast on 33 sts.
- **1st row:** (RS) (k10, p1) 3 times.
- **2nd row:** P1, (k1, p10) twice, k1, p9.
- **3rd row:** (K8, p1, k1, p1) 3 times.
- **4th row:** P1, (k1, p1, k1, p8) twice, k1, p1, k1, p7.
- **5th row:** (K6, [p1, k1] twice, p1) 3 times.
- **6th row:** P1, ([k1, p1] twice, k1, p6) twice, (k1, p1) twice, k1, p5.
- **7th row:** (K4, [p1, k1] 3 times, p1) 3 times.
- **8th row:** P1, ([k1, p1] 3 times, k1, p4) twice, (k1, p1) 3 times, k1, p3.
- **9th row:** (K2, [p1, k1] 4 times, p1) 3 times.
- **10th row:** P1, ([k1, p1] 4 times, k1, p2) twice, (k1, p1)5 times.
- **11th row:** As 10th row.
- **12th row:** P to end.
- **13th-48th rows:** Rep 1st - 12th rows.
- Cast off knitwise, working into the back of each stitch.

MAKING UP

Place the square on a flat, padded surface and ease out to correct dimensions, pinning around edges if necessary. Cover with a clean, lightly dampened cloth and leave until square and cloth are dry. Store the square flat until you are ready to sew the throw together.

For all the abbreviations please refer to the *Practical Guide* on p.52.

19

Square n°60
banded broken rib

Bands of **broken rib** with **stocking stitch** make for a textured square.

MATERIALS

Materials in the box:

- 1 x ball of white yarn (save any leftover for future squares)

Provided in your welcome box:

- A pair of 4mm knitting needles

DIMENSIONS

The finished square measures approx 15 x 15cm.

TENSION

20 sts x 27 rows over 10cm square patt on 4mm needles.

For the best results it is important that you work to stated tension.

HOW TO KNIT THE SQUARE

- ❤ Cast on 30 sts.
- ❤ **1st row:** (RS) k to end.
- ❤ **2nd row:** P to end.
- ❤ Rep 1st and 2nd rows once more to give 4 rows of st st.
- ❤ **5th row:** P to end.
- ❤ **6th row:** P2, *k2, p2, rep from * to end.
- ❤ **7th row:** K2, *p2, k2, rep from * to end.
- ❤ **8th row:** K2, *p2, k2, rep from * to end.
- ❤ **9th row:** P2, *k2, p2, rep from * to end.
- ❤ **10th row:** As 6th row.
- ❤ **11th row:** As 7th row.
- ❤ **12th row:** K to end.
- ❤ Rep these 12 rows twice more.
- ❤ Rep 1st-4th rows.
- ❤ Cast off knitwise working into the back of each st.

MAKING UP

Place the square on a flat, padded surface and ease out to correct dimensions, pinning around edges if necessary. Cover with a clean, lightly dampened cloth and leave until square and cloth are dry. Store the square flat until you are ready to sew the throw together.

TOP TIP

Store the square flat until you are ready to assemble your throw, pin a small piece of paper with the square number on to the square. This will allow you to find your way more easily during the final assembly of your throw.

For all the abbreviations please refer to the *Practical Guide* on p.52.

Audrey *top*

LEVEL ●●○

Understated chic is the hallmark of this **Audrey Hepburn-style** sleeveless top.

MATERIAL

- 5[5:6:6:6] x 50g balls of King Cole Merino Blend DK in main colour (M) – Black (shade 048)
- 1 x 50g ball of Crystal Palace Squiggle in contrast colour (C) – Black-White (shade 9418)
- Pair of 3.25mm needles
- Pair of 4mm needles
- Pair of 5mm needles
- Stitch markers and holders

DIMENSIONS

To fit bust:
81[86:91:97:102]cm.

Actual size:
86[92:97:102.5:108]cm.

Length:
54.5[55.5:55.5:57:58]cm.

Note: Figures in square brackets [ ] refer to larger sizes; where there is only one set of figures, it applies to all sizes.

TENSION

22 sts and 30 rows measure 10cm square over st st using M on 4mm needles.

For the best results it is important that you work to stated tension.

TOP TIP

Knitted in black, this little evening sweater is inspired by Audrey Hepburn. It would look equally chic in other colours.

NEED HELP?

Consult our handy *Getting Started guide* or visit our website at **www.stitch-box.com** for all the tutorials and advice you might need to help you with your knitting projects.

For all the abbreviations please refer to the *Practical Guide* on p.52.

HOW TO KNIT THE TOP

Back

- With 5mm needles and C, cast on 77[81:87:91:95] sts.
- K 4 rows. Beg with a p row, work 9 rows in reverse st st.
- Next row: (WS) k5[2:5:3:0], (inc in next st, k3, inc in next st, k4) 7[8:8:9:10] times, inc in next st, k3, inc in next st, k to end. 93[99:105:111:117] sts. Cut off C and join in M.
- Change to 4mm needles. Beg with a k row, cont in st st throughout and work 2 rows.
- **Dec row:** K15, k2tog tbl, k to last 17 sts, k2tog, k15.
- Work 5 rows straight. Rep last 6 rows until 83[89:95:101:107] sts rem. Work 5 rows straight.
- **Inc row:** K15, m1, k to last 15 sts, m1, k to end.
- Work 9 rows straight. Rep last 10 rows until there are 95[101:107:113:119] sts. Work straight to 37cm from cast-on edge, ending with a p row.
- Insert a marker at centre of last row.

Shape armholes

- Cast off 9[10:9:10:10] sts loosely at beg of next 2 rows. Dec 1 st at each end of next 5[5:7:7:9] rows, then on every foll alt row until 61[65:69:71:73] sts rem. Work straight until armholes measure 13[14:14:14:15]cm from marker, ending with a p row.

Shape neck

- Next row: K15[16:17:17:18], turn and complete this side of neck first.
- **Dec 1 st at neck edge on next 3 rows, then on 2 foll alt rows and finally on foll 4th row. 9[10:11:11:12] sts.
- Work 2[2:2:6:6] rows straight, ending at armhole edge (for other side of neck, work 1 row more here).

Shape shoulder

- Cast off 4[5:5:5:6] sts at beg of next row. Work 1 row. Cast off rem 5[5:6:6:6] sts.
- With RS of work facing, sl centre 31[33:35:37:37] sts on to a holder, rejoin yarn to next st and k to end.
- Complete as first side of neck from ** to end, noting the bracketed exception.

FRONT

Work as given for Back.

Neckband (Work Back and Front alike)

- With 3.25mm needles, M and RS of work facing, pick up and k11[11:11:15:15] sts down one side of neck, k across centre 31[33:35:37:37] sts on holder and pick up and k11[11:11:15:15] sts up other side of neck. 53[55:57:67:67] sts. K 2 rows. Cast off.

Armbands

- Join shoulder and neckband seams.

- With 3.25mm needles, M and RS of work facing, pick up and k98[106:108:116:120] sts evenly around armhole. K 2 rows. Cast off.

MAKING UP

Press, omitting sections in C, following instructions on ball band. Join side and armband seams.

Have fun choosing the yarn for the contrast band at the waist. There are plenty of textured fantasy yarns on the market.

Wire and bead *cuff*

LEVEL ●●○

Knit this **cuff-style bracelet** in **copper wire** and add a sprinkling of glass beads.

MATERIAL

- 1 x reel of 0.351mm supa green coloured copper craft wire (3104)
- Pair of 4mm needles
- 200 x 4mm Czech fire polished glass round beads copper/light sapphire
- 1 medium sized silver-plated toggle clasp set
- Wire cutters or strong everyday scissors

DIMENSIONS

To fit an average-sized woman's wrist.

TENSION

Not critical for this project.

HOW TO KNIT THE WIRE AND BEAD CUFF

Before you begin
(see p. 48-49)

- Thread 200 beads onto the wire.

- Rewind the beaded wire onto the reel, leaving 50cm of wire without beads (to cast on and to attach the toggle clasp). The last bead threaded will be the first bead to be used. The beads are added in a random pattern. As you are knitting with wire you can see the beads from both sides of the knitted fabric, so it does not matter which side the beads are added to. When you want to add a bead, bring the next bead up to the st about to be knitted, then knit the stitch pulling the wire through and so capturing the bead.

For all the abbreviations please refer to the *Practical Guide* on p.52.

Cuff

- Using 4mm needles cast on 20 sts using the non beaded end of the wire.

- Leave a tail of wire to attach the toggle.

- **1st row:** K to end, adding beads as required. Add 2 to 4 beads per row, checking they are not clustered together and have a balanced random feel.

- Rep last row for 60 rows or until cuff fits around wrist taking into account the size of the toggle clasp.

- Cast off, leaving a tail of wire to attach the toggle clasp with.

MAKING UP

To attach the toggle clasp, thread the tail of wire in and out of the cast on sts to the 10th st, this will strengthen the edge. Attach the clasp by threading the wire in and out of the toggle loop. Once secure, thread the rem wire through the other 10 sts. Cut off, making sure the end is hidden and not sharp to the touch. Rep with the other side of the clasp on the other short side of the cuff.

TOP TIP

Knit with craft wire to make fun jewellery. It comes in amazing colours but this green is one of our favourites!

NEED HELP?

Consult our handy *Getting Started guide* or visit our website at **www.stitch-box.com** for all the tutorials and advice you might need to help you with your knitting projects.

Fire polished glass beads are smooth to the touch but sparkle with all kinds of iridescent colours.

Felt *boxes* `LEVEL ●●○`

Like the **famous matryoshka** – Russian stacking dolls – these boxes fit neatly inside each other when empty.

MATERIAL

- 11 x 50g balls of Twilleys Freedom Wool in Garnet (shade 1116)
- 9 x 50g balls in Pearl (shade 1101)
- 2 x 50g balls in Kingfisher (shade 1110)
- Pair of 10mm needles
- Tapestry needle
- Matching sewing thread and needle

DIMENSIONS

Box 1 (Pearl with Garnet flower):

22cm in diameter x 13cm high

Box 2 (Garnet with Pearl flower):

22cm in diameter x 11cm high

Box 3 (Garnet with Pearl flower):

14cm in diameter x 8cm high

Box 4 (Kingfisher with Pearl flower):

9cm in diameter x 7cm high

TENSION

10 sts and 14 rows measure 10cm square over st st on 10mm needles before felting.

For the best results it is important that you work to stated tension.

HOW TO KNIT THE BOXES

BOXES 1 AND 2

Body (make 1 in Pearl and 1 in Garnet)

- ♥ With 10mm needles cast on 30 sts.
- ♥ Work in st st until strip measures 120cm. Cast off.

Circles (make 2 in each of Garnet and Pearl for lids and box bases)

- ♥ With 10mm needles cast on 15 sts. Beg with a k row, cont in st st, inc 1 st at each end of every foll alt row until there are 45 sts.
- ♥ Work straight to 30cm from beg, ending with a p row.
- ♥ Dec 1 st at each end of next and every foll alt row until 15 sts rem. Work 1 row. Cast off.

BOX 3

Body

- ♥ With 10mm needles and Garnet, cast on 22 sts.
- ♥ Work in st st until strip measures 65cm. Cast off.

Lid and base circles (make 2)

- ♥ With 10mm needles and Garnet, cast on 7 sts. Beg with a k row, cont in st st, inc 1 st at each end of every foll alt row until there are 21 sts.
- ♥ Work straight to 14cm from beg, ending with a p row.
- ♥ Dec 1 st at each end of next and every foll alt row until 7 sts rem. Work 1 row. Cast off.

BOX 4

Body

- ♥ With 10mm needles and Kingfisher, cast on 15 sts.
- ♥ Work in st st until strip measures 50cm. Cast off.

Lid and base circles (make 2)

- ♥ With 10mm needles and Kingfisher, cast on 5 sts.
- ♥ Beg with a k row, cont in st st, inc 1 st at each end of every foll alt row until there are 15 sts.
- ♥ Work straight to 10cm from beg, ending with a p row. Dec 1 st at each end of next and every foll alt row until 5 sts rem. Work 1 row. Cast off.

MAKING UP

Felt pieces by washing at 60°C in a machine with a few towels or pairs of jeans for extra agitation. Reshape while still damp and dry flat. Press flat while still slightly damp or after spraying with water. When completely dry, cut pieces to the following dimensions, saving any off-cuts for petals.

Boxes 1 and 2

Lids and bases: 21cm-diameter circles. From each full length body strip, cut the following pieces:

Pearl: 12cm-wide base strip and 3cm-wide lid strip.

Garnet: 10cm-wide base strip and 3cm-wide lid strip.

Box 3

Lid and base: 13cm-diameter circle. From full length body strip, cut the following pieces: 7cm-wide base strip and 4cm-wide lid strip.

NEED HELP?

Consult our handy *Getting Started guide* or visit our website at **www.stitch-box.com** for all the tutorials and advice you might need to help you with your knitting projects.

For all the abbreviations please refer to the *Practical Guide* on p.52.

Box 4

Lid and base: 8cm-diameter circles. From full length body strip, cut the following pieces: 6cm-wide base strip and 3cm-wide lid strip. Now join lid strip to lid circle by positioning raw circle (to make the lid larger than the base) and, using matching sewing thread, sew small, neat zigzag stitches through the felt fabric (there will be small stitches visible on the outer surfaces). Trim the strip to size and join the two ends of strip. Repeat this process to join the base strip to the base circle, placing the raw edge of strip on top of circle (to make box smaller than lid).

Cut five flower petals for each box with lengths of 9cm for box 1, 8cm for box 2, 6cm for box 3 and 4cm for box 4. Arrange the petals so that the points meet in the centre of the lid. Attach each petal with a few stitches through the central tip so that the outer tips can curl upwards slightly. Using contrast coloured yarn and a tapestry needle, sew large cross stitches across the joins on the box and lid as shown. Finally, spray finished box with water, pack with crumpled newspaper then leave to dry to help the boxes maintain their shape.

Tiny bow *necklace*

LEVEL ●○○

Thread a **glittery bow** onto a **velvet ribbon** for a sweet little necklace.

MATERIAL

- 1 x 25g ball of Anchor Metallics yarn in Silver or Gold)
- Pair of 2.25mm needles
- 30cm length of 3mm wide velvet ribbon or chain
- Small brooch pin (optional)
- Sewing needle and matching thread
- Yarn needle

DIMENSIONS

Small: 4cm across; **Medium:** 5cm across **Large:** 6cm across

Note: Figures in square brackets [ ] refer to larger sizes; where there is only one set of figures, it applies to all sizes.

TENSION

30 sts and 40 rows measure 10cm square over st st on 2.25mm needles.

For the best results it is important that you work to stated tension.

HOW TO KNIT THE BOWS

- Using 2.25mm needles, cast on 10[12:16] sts.

- Work in st st for 15[19:25] rows ending with a RS row.

- **Next row:** K to create a fold line.

- Cont in st st until both sides of the fold line are equal in length.

- Cast off.

TOP TIP

Anchor have a huge range of metallic yarns in jewel-like bright colours.

NEED HELP?

Consult our handy *Getting Started guide* or visit our website at **www.stitch-box.com** for all the tutorials and advice you might need to help you with your knitting projects.

For all the abbreviations please refer to the *Practical Guide* on p.52.

MAKING UP

Fold over and stitch along all open seams using mattress stitch. Sew in all loose ends. Take a length of yarn and stitch a row of running stitch across the centre of the stitched rectangle. Gather this and tie off. Using 2.25mm needles, cast on 4[5:7] sts. Work in st st until piece fits around the gathered centre of the bow when slightly stretched. Cast off and stitch in place around the centre of the bow. Take a small length of ribbon and thread it through the centre of the bow.

Although this is a metallic yarn it is soft and easy to work with on small needles.

The large bow can be made into a brooch by stitching the brooch pin to the back.

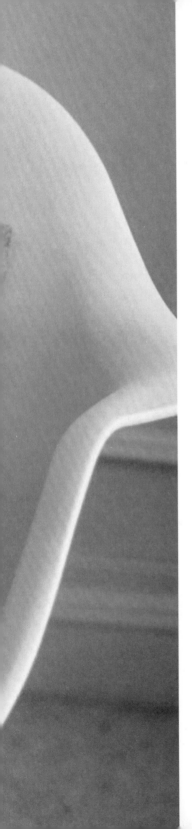

Penguin *cushion*

LEVEL ●●○

Pick up this **cute little fella** and pop him on a chair, sofa or bed.

MATERIAL

- 2 x 100g balls of Katia Peru in: A - Silver (shade 29)
- 1 x 100g ball in each of the following shades:
  B – Charcoal (shade 13)
  C – Cream (shade 3)
  D – Orange (shade 22)
- Pair of 6mm needles
- 40 x 40cm cushion pad
- 4 stitch markers
- Yarn needle

DIMENSIONS

42 x 42cm.

TENSION

13 sts x 17 rows measure 10cm square over st st on 6mm needles.

For the best results it is important that you work to stated tension.

Note: The penguin motif is worked using the intarsia method. Wind off small balls of yarn to work each section. We would recommend Swiss darning (duplicate stitch) the eyes and beak on at the making up stage, which will make it a lot easier to manage the yarn. When working the chart, RS rows are worked from right to left and WS rows from left to right.

HOW TO KNIT THE CUSHION

- Using 6mm needles and A, cast on 52 sts.
- **1st row:** (RS) k to end.
- **2nd row:** P to end.
- Rep 1st and 2nd rows a further 3 times.

Commence working from chart as foll:

- **1st row:** K8, PM, work 1st row from chart, PM, k to end.
- **2nd row:** P to marker, SM, work 2nd row from chart, SM, p to end.
- **3rd row:** K to marker, SM, work 3rd row from chart, SM, k to end.
- Cont working from chart as set until all 55 rows have been worked.
- Using A only, cont working in st st (starting with a p row) as set until work measures 40cm from cast-on edge. PM at beg and end of this row (fold line).
- Using yarn A only, cont working in st st as set until work measures 40cm from markers.
- Cast off.

MAKING UP

Darn in all ends and block. Swiss darn the beak and eyes using the chart Fold at the fold-line and sew the side seams using mattress stitch. Insert the cushion pad and mattress stitch the bottom seam.

TOP TIP

This yarn is a great blend of acrylic, wool and alpaca and it has good stitch definition, which makes it perfect for an intarsia project like this.

Swiss darn the eyes and beak following the chart for the correct position.

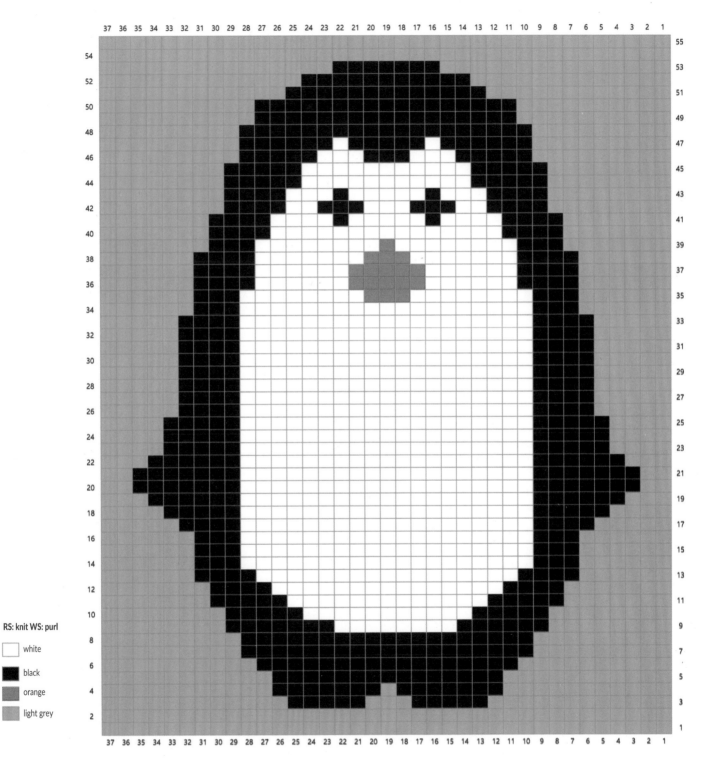

RS: knit WS: purl

- ☐ white
- ■ black
- ■ orange
- ■ light grey

Squared *checks*

This pattern gives an overall appearance of **squares-within-squares**. The smaller **stocking stitch squares** in the centre of the blocks also look as if they are threaded through the fabric. Clever stuff!

HOW TO WORK THE PATTERN

This is how the instructions for Squared checks would be given in a pattern:

- ❤ **1st row:** (RS) k to end.
- ❤ **2nd row:** P to end.
- ❤ **3rd row:** K2, *p8, k2, rep from * to end.
- ❤ **4th row:** P2, *k8, p2, rep from * to end.
- ❤ **5th row:** K2, *p2, k4, p2, k2, rep from * to end.
- ❤ **6th row:** P2, *k2, p4, k2, p2, rep from * to end.
- ❤ **7th-10th rows:** Rep 5th and 6th rows twice.
- ❤ **11th and 12th rows:** As 3rd and 4th rows.

These twelve rows form the pattern and are repeated for a certain number of repeats or a given measurement.

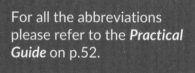

For all the abbreviations please refer to the *Practical Guide* on p.52.

NEED HELP?

Consult our handy *Getting Started guide* or visit our website at **www.stitch-box.com** for all the tutorials and advice you might need to help you with your knitting projects.

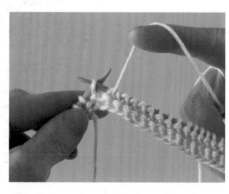

① Cast on the required number of stitches. The pattern is worked over multiples of ten stitches plus two. Knit the first row, which is the right side, and purl the second.

TOP TIP

The pattern is worked over twelve rows, and has a general stocking stitch background with larger squares of reverse stocking stitch and then, within these, smaller squares of stocking stitch.

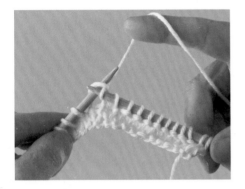

2 For the third row, knit two and then repeat a sequence of purl eight and knit two to the end of the row.

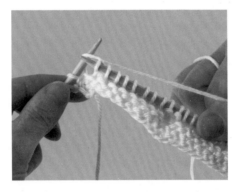

3 For row four, purl two and then knit eight and purl two. Repeat this knit and purl sequence to the end of the row.

4 Begin the fifth row with knit two, then work a sequence of purl two, knit four, purl two and knit two and repeat this to the end of the row.

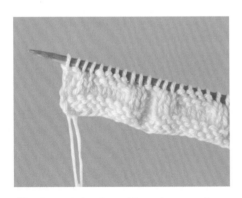

5 Row six begins with purl two and then a knit two, purl four, knit two, purl two sequence is repeated to the end of the row.

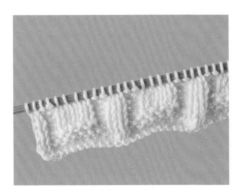

6 Repeat rows five and six twice more. This completes the tenth row of the pattern.

7 To finish the twelve-row pattern, repeat rows three and four. This is how the first pattern repeat will look.

Mosaic *stitch*

Rope-like ribs give this stitch its **distinctive appearance** although it does not have the elasticity of a true rib stitch.

NEED HELP?

Consult our handy *Getting Started guide* or visit our website at **www.stitch-box.com** for all the tutorials and advice you might need to help you with your knitting projects.

For all the abbreviations please refer to the *Practical Guide* on p.52.

HOW TO WORK THE PATTERN

This is how the instructions for Mosaic stitch would be given in a pattern:

- ❤ **1st row:** (RS) p3, *k1, p3, k1, p1, k1, p3, rep from * to last 4 sts, k1, p3.
- ❤ **2nd row:** K3, *p1, k3, p1, k1, p1, k3, rep from * to last 4 sts, p1, k3.
- ❤ **3rd row:** As 1st row.
- ❤ **4th row:** As 2nd row.
- ❤ **5th row:** P2, *k1, p1, k1, p3, k1, p3, rep from * to last 5 sts k1, p1, k1, p2.
- ❤ **6th row:** K2, *p1, k1, p1, k3, p1, k3, rep from * to last 5 sts, p1, k1, p1, k2.
- ❤ **7th row:** As 5th row.
- ❤ **8th row:** As 6th row.

These eight rows form the pattern and are repeated for a given number of times or for a certain measurement.

TOP TIP

The pattern is worked over eight rows and features a rib that alternates between single and double vertical rows of knit stitches to form a chain-like pattern.

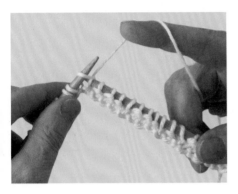

1 Cast on the required number of stitches. The pattern is worked over a repeat of ten stitches plus seven. For the first row, which is the right side, begin with purl three. Work the following sequence: knit one, purl three, knit one, purl one, knit one, purl three. Repeat this to the last four stitches and then knit one and purl three.

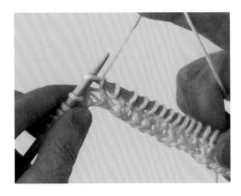

2 Begin the second row with knit three. Work the following sequence: purl one, knit three, purl one, knit one, purl one, knit three. Repeat this to the last four stitches and then purl one and knit three.

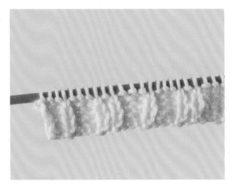

3 For the third and fourth row, repeat the first and second rows.

4 For the fifth row, purl two and then work a sequence of knit one, purl one, knit one, purl three, knit one, purl three to the last five stitches. Knit one, purl one, knit one, purl two.

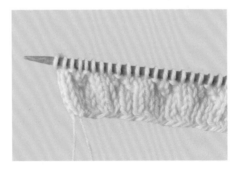

5 Begin the sixth row with knit two. Work the following sequence: purl one, knit one, purl one, knit three, purl one, knit three. Repeat to the last five stitches then purl one, knit one, purl one, knit two.

6 For the seventh and eighth row, repeat the fifth and sixth rows. This completes the first pattern repeat.

Fern *lace*

In this delicate lace pattern, **vertical lines** of holes are linked by **diagonal rows** of stocking stitch that resemble **fern leaves**. It is an ideal lace stitch for using as an all-over pattern.

NEED HELP?

Consult our handy *Getting Started guide* or visit our website at **www.stitch-box.com** for all the tutorials and advice you might need to help you with your knitting projects.

HOW TO WORK THE PATTERN

This is how the instructions for Fern lace would be given in a pattern:

- **1st row:** (WS) p to end.
- **2nd row:** K3, *yfwd, k2, sl 1, k1, psso, k2tog, k2, yfwd, k1, rep from * to last st, k1.
- **3rd row:** P to end.
- **4th row:** K2, *yfwd, k2, sl 1, k1, psso, k2tog, k2, yfwd, k1, rep from * to last 2 sts, k2.

These four rows form the pattern and are repeated for a certain number of repeats or a given measurement.

TOP TIP

The pattern is worked over four rows and it is not a difficult pattern to follow because, although the increases and decreases are made at different places in the row, the overall number of stitches remain the same.

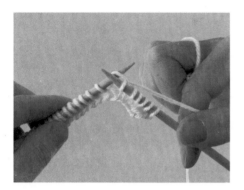

1. Cast on the required number of stitches. The pattern is worked over multiples of nine stitches plus four. For the first row, which is the wrong side, purl to the end. Begin the second row with knit three, then bring the yarn forward, and knit two stitches.

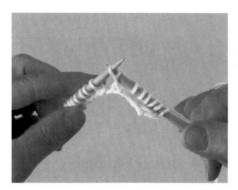

2. Slip the next stitch, knit one and then pass the slipped stitch over the knit stitch and off the righthand needle.

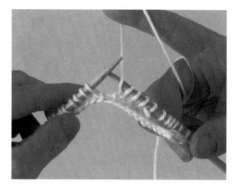

3. Knit the next two stitches together, knit two stitches, bring the yarn forward and knit one.

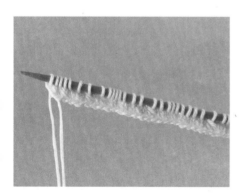

4. Repeat this sequence from the first yarn forward instruction to the last stitch on the row and then knit one.

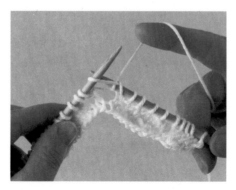

5. For the third row, purl to the end. Begin the fourth row by knitting two stitches. Work a sequence of yarn forward, knit two, slip one stitch and knit one stitch, pass the slipped stitch over the knit stitch and then knit two stitches together, knit two, yarn forward and knit one.

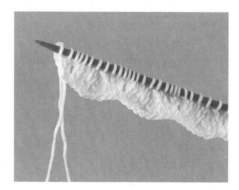

6. Repeat this sequence to the last two stitches and then knit two. You will begin to see the lace pattern emerging as you complete the first pattern repeat. Continue to work 1st to 4th rows.

Knitting *with beads*
(between two stitches)

There are several different ways to knit with beads and here we look at the method known as **bead knitting**, which places each bead between two stitches. Before you begin, you will need to **thread the beads** onto the working yarn.

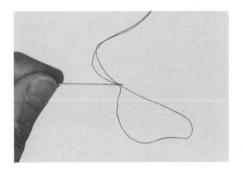

1. Unless you are using beads with a very large hole it will not be possible to thread the beads directly onto the yarn. This is how you thread them onto the yarn and this has to be done before you begin knitting. Thread a sewing needle with ordinary sewing thread but thread it with both ends of the thread so you have a loop of thread, as shown.

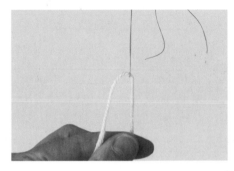

2. Take the yarn that you want to thread the beads onto and pass the end through the loop of sewing thread.

KNITTING SOS

This beading technique was traditionally used for making purses and therefore it is sometimes known as purse knitting. It was very popular in the 18th century.

3. Pass the first bead over the end of the needle and push it down over the sewing thread and then over the yarn.

4. Continue in this way, bead by bead, until you have all the beads you will need on the yarn. Remove the loop of sewing thread and needle and cast on in the usual way. As you work you can push each bead up the yarn as it is required.

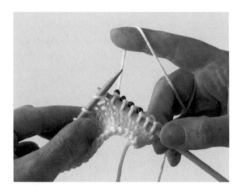

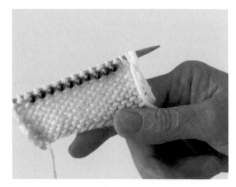

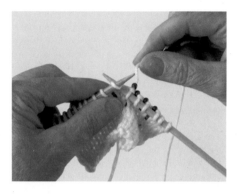

5 Cast on and work in stocking stitch until you reach the position for the first bead. If this is on a knit row, the beads will sit on the purl side of the work. Place the right-hand needle into the next stitch on the left needle and then slide the bead up as close to the knitting as possible. Work the next stitch and continue in this way to position each bead.

6 Work to the end of the row. Each bead is positioned between two stitches.

7 Work a purl row and then on the next knit row, continue placing the beads.

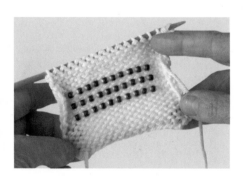

8 This is how the beads will look if they are worked on alternative knit rows and placed in the same position, one above the other.

9 To place the beads on the knit rows, slide the beads up into position on the purl rows.

10 Once each bead is in position, push it through to the knit side of the work.

Smocking

Smocking is familiar on fabric especially **children's garments**. It works equally well with knitted ribbed fabrics. Use the **same colour yarn** or a **contrasting colour** for the smocking stitches.

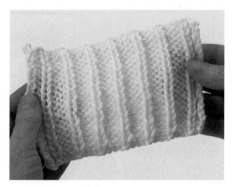

1 Our example here uses a piece of purl three, knit one fabric. The smocking is worked from left to right and the smocking stitches are spaced on every fourth row in a zigzag fashion.

2 Thread a blunt-ended needle with yarn for the smocking stitches. Bring the needle through to the front of the fabric just to the left of the knit rib. Follow the row across and take the needle under the next rib from right to left.

KNITTING SOS

The rib should not be too wide or the fabric will be too bulky when it is pulled together by the smocking stitches. A p3, k1 rib or p4, k1 is ideal to form the smocked pattern.

3 Follow the row back and take the needle under the stitch that forms the first rib, from right to left, bringing it out next to the original entry point.

4 Pull the stitch gently so that the ribs lie next to each other.

5 Make two more smocking 6 stitches by taking the needle into the side of the right-hand rib and bringing it out at the side of the left hand rib and then repeating this.

6 Count four rows up and then bring the yarn back to the front at the left hand side of the second knit rib.

7 Follow the row across and then take the needle under the third rib from right to left. Take the needle back across the row and under the second rib.

8 Pull the yarn gently to bring the 9 two ribs together so that they lie flat and side by side. Repeat step 5 to complete the second smocking stitch.

9 Count down four rows and work the next set of smocking stitches opposite the first set by joining the third and fourth ribs.

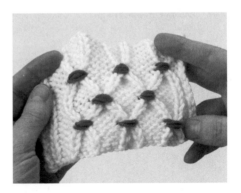

10 Continue in this way working in a zigzag pattern across the ribs until you have completed the required number of smocking stitches.

Practical Guide

Here you will find the abbreviations and basic techniques most frequently used in our pattern instructions.

LIST OF ABBREVIATIONS

alt	alternate, alternately		**RS**	right side (front of work)
beg	beginning		**st**	stitch(es)
cm	centimetre(s)		**tog**	together
CO	cast on		**WS**	wrong side (back of work)
cont	continue			
dec	decrease, decreasing			
foll	following			
g	gram(s)			
inc	increase, increasing			
k	knit			
m	metre(s)			
p	purl			
rem	remaining			
rep	repeat			
rnd	round			

GUIDES

You will find additional guides like this at the end of each book covering any abbreviations and techniques specific to that month's patterns. More complex techniques — which can be used to add decorative holes or to make textured patterns in your work — will be explained as they are introduced to our patterns.